Olivia's Question

by

Lori Freudenberg

Illustrations by Sara Lindner

Illustrations by Sara Lindner

ISBN: 978-1-949565-32-4

Dedicated to
Gerry
Thank you for your encouragement and love
And to
Olivia Jo
You stole my heart!

Where was I and what was I before I became me?

Was I a flower in the field swaying gently in the breeze?

Was I the breeze swooping down from the tall, green trees?

Was I a drop of water in the ocean
as it broke upon the beach?

Was I a grain of the sand or
a ripe, juicy peach?

Was I a bird in the sky on a sunny, cloudless day?

Was I a bee spreading pollen from the flowers bloomed in May?

"Yes," cried the Lord from
Their place inside my heart.
"Yes, can't you see we've been one from the start?

Every living thing that you hear and touch and see,
Every living thing is connected back to "We."

For you and I and everything are one,
through and through.
It matters not our race, our age,
our beliefs or what we do.

We are one, don't you see,
it's most important that you know.

We are one, don't you see,
and from this knowledge will now flow:

Kindness in your deeds and words,
for that brings peace across the lands.

Feel the joy in every heart as
you join your precious hands.

For you, my dear, are everything,
the flowers and the trees,
the sand, the bird, the peach and
the water in the seas.

Remember you are everything
and every other living thing is too.
And if you remember that, my love,
you will bloom in all you do!

Where were you and what were you before
you became you?
You were everywhere and everything,
and everything else was too."